Find & Keep Your Happy

Tamika Andrea

Find & Keep Your Happy

Copyright © 2020 by Tamika A. Johnson. All rights reserved. Printed in the United States of America. No parts of this book may be used or reproduced in any manner whatsoever without written permission except in the case of brief quotations embodied in critical articles and reviews.

If you would like permission to use the material from the book, please contact the author. Thank you for your support of the author's right.

Scriptures quotations noted NIV are taken from the Holy Bible, New International Version®, NIV®. Copyright © 1973, 1978, 1984, 2011 by Biblica, Inc.™ Used by permission of Zondervan. All rights reserved.

Scriptures quotations noted KJV are taken from the King James Version of the Bible.

Published, formatted and interior designed by E.Stones, LLC
www.estonesllc.com

Edited by Kimberli Wilson

ISBN: 978-1-7349985-0-4

Find & Keep
Your Happy

"When you pass through the waters, I will be with you; and when you pass through the rivers, they will not sweep over you. When you walk through the fire, you will not be burned; the flames will not set you ablaze."
Isaiah 43:2 NIV

DEDICATION

To My #1 Supporter, My Hero, My Mentor and biggest Fan who is now my Heavenly Angel, My Father Lemuel Houston Jr. To say that I miss you is an understatement. I treasure every lesson you've given me and the footprints you left for me to follow. You were my WHY for so many years and still to this day I just want to make you proud. The pain of not having you here physically has been unbearable some days, and I constantly ask God if I can just have you back. The inability to pick up the phone to call you to share or celebrate each of my accomplishments has been bittersweet. There were many times that I wanted to say forget it all, but I could hear you saying "Keep Going Mika, You've Got This Babe."

I'm reminded daily that I was raised by the best; therefore, born for success and I couldn't give up if I wanted to. You were the epitome of a King and a Father and it's because of your love and the strength you instilled in me that I am finally able to share my journey with the world. I love you Daddy.

TABLE OF CONTENTS

Chapter 1	*The Beginning*	1
Chapter 2	*Hell & High Water*	13
Chapter 3	*Pushing Pass the Past*	36
Chapter 4	*Overcoming*	45
Chapter 5	*Daddy Knows Best*	56
Chapter 6	*Holy NOTrimony*	70
Chapter 7	*Tragedy & Trials*	82
Chapter 8	*A Look in the Mirror*	90
Chapter 9	*The New YOU: Push, Pull & Strive*	95

In Remembrance of ….	*100*
Acknowledgements	*102*
About the Author	*106*

Chapter 1
The Beginning

Pulling back the layers and reflecting on your past.. where it all started. Revisiting your childhood & many contributions to your now.

The things that take place during your childhood, whether good or bad are a part of you forever. You carry those memories, wounds, and moments with you throughout life. Reflecting on your past can be painful but it's purposeful. Your past is deeply rooted within you, it's who you are, where you come from and plays a pivotal role in your adulthood, relationships etc.

As a child, life is just simple, stress free, full of joy, toys and ice cream. The sky is beautiful and filled with clouds and everyone around you is happy, smiling and full of life. I can't remember which book I read or what commercial flashed across the television that painted this "beautiful picture" of such a fairytale childhood, but it surely wasn't mine.

I lived in Laclede Town in Saint. Louis, MO with my mother and her boyfriend. The sky as I saw it was always dark, and I rarely saw a smiling face in our home. As a little girl you dream a lot. You may dream of being a princess like Cinderella, a mermaid like Arielle, a doctor or maybe even a big-time defense attorney as I once did. At the tender age of four all I dreamt and wished for was to never again witness my mother's boyfriend punch her in the nose so hard that it starts to bleed.

I was a very independent child and I loved my mother deeply. She was so beautiful; her smile and pretty white teeth completed the package.

As a little girl I knew I wanted to do something that involved talking and helping people. Becoming an attorney was my first choice and I was sure I wanted to be an Evangelist just like my grandmother. Either way, I just had to be amongst people and do something impactful. My Dad was my hero and I watched him very closely. I am certain I received my entrepreneurial eye, pure heart of genuine love and eagerness to help others from him. My Dad actually dressed me in little business suits and "Sunday dresses" all the time. Picture this little girl with two-piece suits, purses and sometimes a little briefcase. When I got older, I enjoyed looking at my pictures and would ask my grandmother whom I call Gany, "Why was I always dressed like every day was Easter?" she really didn't have an answer for me besides "Mika honey, your Daddy dresses you." Nonetheless, family was always important to me and even as a kid I always wanted to make sure everyone else was okay.

My father was very active in my life. I couldn't wait until Friday rolled around as I knew my dad would bring me gifts when he came to pick me up from school and he would even bring treats for my classmates. Weekends with him were nothing short of amazing. Some would say that my dad spoiled me. All I knew was that I absolutely adored him, and he supported all of my crazy aspirations. I also looked forward to spending time with my oldest sister, we would go to my grandparents' house to help work in their garden. I remember my Dad dressing my older sister and I in pretty dresses often and making every day feel like Christmas with dolls, toys and whatever we wanted. My older sister and I didn't share the same mother, but we were very close and would both spend every weekend with our dad.

In addition to spending time with my dad and sister over the weekends, I spent time with my older cousin, on my Dad's side, she was one of my idols. I remember the first time we went shopping with her boyfriend's mother and instead of buying toys or candy, like most kids, I purchased my first single cassette tape "I don't wanna fight" by my favorite entertainer Ms. Tina Turner.

They all lived in Cahokia, IL near my Dad. I guess you could say it was something like a fairytale come true "get away" weekend which I never took for granted. I realized that my weekends with my dad were pretty much my peace at a difficult time during my childhood. I went to school from my mother's house during the week and my dad never missed a weekend picking me up.

At home it was me, my mother and her boyfriend and there was no fairytale to say the least. My mother was always a hard worker, she worked at one of the most prestigious hotels in St. Louis in the housekeeping department. She was constantly recognized for her phenomenal work ethic. Our routine was the same every day, school for me, work for her and her boyfriend had three jobs; to sell drugs, use them and to find something to argue and fight with my mother about. I witnessed my mother crying so much and although he never laid a hand on me, he made sure I was in the room to see him put his hands on my mother. If I spoke up or stared him down like the devil he was; he would then send me to my room and tell me not to come out.

One day while in my room playing with my barbie dolls, I heard her let out a scream from the pits of her stomach. I ran out of my room and saw her nose bleeding and her left eye red, swollen and nearly shut. Although what I really wanted to do was find the nearest hammer and black his eye and break his nose, instead I ran to my room and grabbed the first thing I could find which were a pair of my underwear out of my drawer. I rushed back to her and started to clean her nose. As I rubbed her back and told her "it's gonna be okay mama." He yelled out "get yo lil a$$ back in that room... this is between me and your mama." I remember not sleeping much in that apartment and worrying a lot. I was just four-years-old and every day I thought about running away, but I kept hearing a voice telling me that everything will be okay--just stand still.

I was barely in kindergarten and to most not nearly old enough to understand the gist of everything that was happening around me, but I did understand and often blamed myself for not being able to rescue my mother and stop all the physical and mental abuse she endured. I could barely play with my friends and focus on the fun activities in pre-K because I would be so worried that one day I would come home from school and my mom would have taken her life.

Each day on the short distance home from school, which was right across the parking lot from our apartment, I never knew what to expect. Some days I would have a chance to play jump rope with my friends and other days I found myself helping my neighbor pick up her mother's belongings that were scattered across the parking lot after being thrown out of the car by her boyfriend. Let's just say I really never knew what a dull day was because there was always an action movie going on around me, except we weren't at a movie theatre. One snowy night while my mother and I were carrying in groceries, we heard screams coming from behind the neighbor's car. As we approached, we could see a trail of blood in the snow. My mother yelled out "get your g** da** hands off of her" while charging towards our neighbor's boyfriend as if she was ready to tear his head off of his shoulders with her bare hands. I could hear our neighbor's daughter, who at the time was maybe seven or eight years old; screaming and crying at the top of her lungs. As I ran up to where my mom was, I saw this man literally stomping our neighbor in the head while wearing huge heavy boots. I watched my mother who was determined to pull him off of her and I noticed there was blood everywhere. There was so much rage in his eyes, my mother used her body weight and was able to nearly knock this six-foot man off his feet, she then yelled "Hit me you coward...I bet you won't hit me." He hopped in his car and fled, not knowing if he had beat this woman to death and not caring to even look back. I could visibly see blood pouring from the area near our neighbor's neck so I removed my scarf and held it up to her neck. She tried to open her eyes, her face was full of blood and he had ripped off her clothes in the freezing cold and snow.

My mother was screaming for help and urging someone to call the police. She didn't have a phone, so we began ringing every apartment's doorbell and knocking on windows. We were trembling, crying and completely in a state of shock. When we finally heard sirens, the ambulance came full speed through our apartment complex. I remember my mom waving them down; we were standing there cold, shivering and covered in blood and all I could think was, "Lord please don't take her mommy away from her."

They took her to the hospital and a relative arrived to get her daughter. A few weeks passed and she was released from the hospital with fractured bones and permanent jaw damage but Thank God she was alive. Even at the age of four, I was no stranger to prayer. I remember praying the night the incident took place and begging God to save her life and keep that demon of a man away from her and her daughter. I overheard her tell my mother she would never take him back after he almost killed her and she would never put her daughter through that again.

About a month later, while outside jumping rope after school I saw that long brown car turn into the parking lot. When the door swung open and that huge boot hit the ground, I could not believe this monster was back. Moments later our neighbor came out wearing a pretty dress and holding flowers up to her nose that I assumed he brought for her, and they pulled off. As a child I didn't understand how a person can beat you for breakfast, lunch and dinner repeatedly for years, throw you out of their car onto the ground covered in snow, nearly take your life in front of your child and you forgive them and take them back.

I also didn't understand how outside of our home my mother was known to protect herself, stand toe to toe and even fist fight with any man, but allowed her boyfriend who was at most a hundred and fifty pounds soak and wet to randomly punch her in the face. It wasn't even prompted by something that she did, it was because he thought another guy looked at her too long while we were at the grocery store or gas station. He was very jealous. My mother was beautiful inside and out with an outgoing personality that people loved; I think he hated that. He had recently returned home from serving a ten-year prison sentence. I remember going with her to visit him, at that point he was the total opposite; nice, always smiling and gentle. When he first came home, he was helpful around the house, offering to help with homework, a very intelligent man, but after a while it was like a dark cloud came in.

    I spent a lot of time with my aunt, my mom's sister. I was with her so much that people started to think she was my mom. She and I were almost the same complexion and she was just as beautiful as both my mom and grandmother. When my mother worked late, my aunt came over to watch me. One evening while my aunt was sitting at the dining room table polishing her nails, I was in the room playing with my dolls and I just began to cry. I began thinking about everything that happens once my aunt leaves and my mother's boyfriend comes home. I was so tired of seeing my mom cry when I knew how strong she was. I saw a book of matches on my mother's night stand and I ripped one off. I'd never even touched matches or even a lighter, so I don't even know why I picked them up. I began striking it until it lit, and the match fell out of my hand and hit the floor. I screamed as I realized the carpet was on fire. I panicked and jumped up and locked the door, but my aunt could already smell the smoke. She was banging at the door demanding I open it. I told her I was so sorry and I didn't want to get a whooping. I screamed through the door "I accidentally set the carpet on fire" she said "You did what?? Girl you better open this door" The flame grew bigger and bigger so I opened the door and ran out. My aunt was able to put the fire out and thankfully no one was hurt. I knew better than to do something so foolish and careless, but I guess I was trying to get attention or maybe trying to make someone realize that my mom and I were living a total nightmare. I knew that anything was better than what we were waking up to everyday and I just wanted to be rescued. My aunt never knew of the severity of the situation at our house, my mother never spoke to anyone about it and neither did I.

    Seeing my mother constantly come to our neighbor's rescue confused me a little, mainly because she couldn't come to her own rescue. I watched her weaken more and more every day in that apartment. I watched him snatch her dignity with every punch. I cried myself to sleep many nights and I told my mother if she wasn't going to leave him, I wanted to move in with my dad. She refused to leave him. That summer, I went to spend the weekend with my grandmother instead of my dad and although I didn't share with her exactly what was going on, she sensed something wasn't right at home. My grandmother was an

Evangelist and like my mother she was beautiful. She had really long black hair that she wore pinned up most times. When I was at her house, I went to church with her and visited the homes of severely ill elders. She prayed, cooked, cleaned and cared for them. She taught me to pray and trust God no matter what. One weekend before I left, she said "Mika I want you to pack your bag and have it ready on Friday I'm coming to get you," I knew she didn't mean she was just coming to get me as she's done before and bringing me back on Sunday night--I knew she meant for good.

    That particular week things had gotten worse; my mother's lip was swollen, and she didn't talk as much as she once did when we were home. Her boyfriend's drug habit worsened, and so did the fighting and arguing. Friday came and I was ready when my grandmother arrived. That was my last night in Laclede Town. My grandmother actually lived in a pretty rough neighborhood called Walnut Park on the northside of St Louis, but anything was better than the nightmare I was in. I missed my mother so much and part of me wanted to go back just to be with her; but the truth is as strong as my mother was her weakness was not only her boyfriend--it became crack cocaine as well.

Me at 5-years-old

Trust in the LORD with all thine heart; and lean not unto thine own understanding. In all thy ways acknowledge him, and he shall direct thy paths.
Proverbs 3:5-6 KJV
My Gany's Favorite Scripture

Chapter 2
Hell & High Water

This is where you reflect on some of "The first storms" in your life...what should've killed you BUT God covered you... Facing what has weighed you down & stopped your growth.

"They say" trials and storms come to make you strong" but what do you say to a child who's weathering all those storms alone? I'm sure you can think of the times you endured your heaviest storms and wasn't quite sure how you would make it through, BUT GOD. Sometimes it's very difficult to face what once weighed you down, but let's celebrate the fact that it no longer has a hold on you.

I had an extremely supportive father and a praying grandmother who cared for me, but there was nothing like a mother's love. I continued to pray for my mother every night as I got settled at my grandparent's house for good. It was bittersweet for a while but as time passed, I learned to deal with the circumstances.

My mom didn't come to pick me up or even put up a fight with my grandmother to get me back because she knew I was in much better hand. I knew she truly didn't want me to see her in her weakest moments, she knew she wasn't able to rise above them just yet. My dad still picked me up every other weekend as he had always done, but I began to see less and less of my mother. My mom and dad were actually married when they were teenagers, but they separated shortly before I was born. I attended Walbridge Elementary, two blocks from my grandmother's house. I was so excited to start school in a new environment. I was looking forward to making new friends and just being a regular kid. I absolutely loved school and never wanted to miss a day, not even when I was sick. I quickly made friends at school, and immediately recognized one who would eventually become my best friend.

In Walnut Park there was much more exposure to things I had never actually seen, except in a movie maybe. Two of my friends and I walked to school together every morning and met up with our other friend that lived right across from the school. My best friend's mother dropped her and her sister off at school. Their grandparents lived one block away from us and we would play after school and on the weekends. During our walks to school we would see pipes on the ground. That reminded me of the ones my mother's boyfriend used; I would see them on the table at my mother's house in Laclede Town. We witnessed drugs being exchanged for money right outside the store we stopped to get donuts from some mornings. This didn't stop us from walking to school every day or playing double dutch outside after school. We just wanted to be kids. Two of my friends were sisters and as we bonded and grew closer, I learned that we had more in common than we thought; their mom had a drug addiction and they also lived with their grandmother. I always kept a smile on my face. I loved my family; I loved my neighborhood and I LOVED school. If I were sick, I would tell my grandmother I felt fine just so I didn't have to miss a day of school. I always made honor roll and if there was an afterschool program, my friends and I were definitely there. In the middle of the school year, my two friends' mom tragically overdosed and passed away. That was certainly not the easiest thing to deal with at all, especially since that was what I feared most for my mom.

  As children we were forced to deal with things most kids our age had never even seen in a movie, yet it was our reality. Our neighborhood was rough, so much so that even a drive by shooting no longer startled us. We had become immune to it. When you're that young and your life is transitioning at such a fast pace, it's kind of frightening so you tend to focus on anything that keeps you smiling and poses a distraction to keep your mind off of the bad. Although I hadn't seen my mom on a consistent basis, when I was in the second grade, I learned that she was pregnant with twins and I was super excited about becoming a big sister. She was still with the boyfriend from hell and she missed every honor roll ceremony and every speech I gave for black history month or entrepreneur day. When other kids' parents would come eat breakfast with them or walk them to class I just stared, stayed quiet and wished my mom would either come walking through the door or was waiting outside when school let out. My grandmother was there whenever her schedule allowed, but she traveled a lot as an evangelist and my grandfather worked.

    As time passed, I became more and more involved in school activities, during the school day and after. I was seven years old in the second grade and had just made it home from African dance class when my grandmother informed me that my mother would be moving in with her boyfriend's grandmother who literally lived three doors down from us on the same side of the street. I was happy to hear that because I hadn't seen my mother in quite some time, but I wasn't happy about seeing her boyfriend of course. I'd overheard a few conversations between my grandmother and my aunt. I also heard my grandmother praying with other ministers over the phone several times for my mother. So, I had an idea that she wasn't doing any better since the last time I'd seen her. They moved in, and I was now a big sister to a twin brother and sister. It was awkward because my mother was now a few houses down from me yet more distant than she was before she moved closer. She even looked different. The abuse and drugs clearly had begun to take a toll on her, there were marks on her face and she'd lost a tremendous amount of weight. She was still a beautiful woman, but she had lost the glow that I had grown accustomed to seeing all over her. Her boyfriend was working for an asphalt company. Unfortunately, his money would be gone by the evening of pay day. He basically worked to support his habit and my mother got whatever was left over to take care of herself and my brother and sister.

  After a while, she did begin to show up at my school occasionally during breakfast or lunch. By this time everyone in the neighborhood who knew our family, could tell my mother was not the woman she used to be and that crack cocaine made its way into her life in a heavy way. I dreamt that my mother would walk me to school, eat lunch with me and get to know my teachers. However, I'll admit I was a little embarrassed because it wasn't her, she wasn't the fun beautiful lady with a smile worth a million dollars at that point.

She once dressed in some of the nicest garments, wore makeup, expensive perfume and every strand of her hair was always in place. According to the pictures I saw, she and my dad complimented each other well. They were both always sharp from head to toe. She really was something like a supermodel before my brothers and sisters' dad was released from prison. My mother was still my mother, yet it was like she had forgotten about me and there was simply no connection between us. She never asked how my day went, she didn't show up for any parent teacher conferences, she never saw a page of my homework and I can't remember us exchanging "I love you's" during that time. I knew firsthand what others didn't and the pain she'd endured for many years, but I went through the pain too; it ripped my heart apart every time blood was on her face and watching her fall apart before my eyes. I had grown accustomed to her being a beautiful strong woman, and quickly realized how life's challenges tend to strip a person of everything if you allow it to.

My brother and my sister were getting big, I would drop my backpack off at home and go down the street to check on them and most times my mother was nowhere to be found. She would be gone for days and never call to even let anyone know that she was okay. My grandmother made sure I took food for the kids to eat and I would get them dressed or whatever was needed. They were often there with their great grandmother and male cousin. I visited them sometimes when my grandmother was out of town. Their male cousin always seemed weird to me and made me feel uncomfortable. He babysat my brothers and sister for my mom from time to time. I always checked on them and sometimes stayed until either their father came home or my mother turned up. The cousin was quiet and smiled a lot, he was always nice to us but there was still something off about him. My mom's boyfriend had an older son and he became a big brother to me too, he came to visit off and on. He lived a few blocks over from us with his grandparents as he'd lost his mom at a very young age.

People sent for my grandmother to come out of town a lot and she would be gone for weeks at a time for revivals. I went with her throughout the summer and I was told by many that I was just as anointed as she was. I would pray and lay hands on people and help my grandmother wash their feet, whatever was needed is what my grandmother provided. She was so beautiful and so loved by many. We drove state to state for two weeks once doing nightly revivals and loads of people drove from other states and found their way to our hotel room just so she could anoint them and give them a word from the Lord. I saw miracles performed; I saw the sick literally get healed all at the hands of my grandmother. I didn't know her title aside from being an evangelist was a "prophet", honestly, I just thought she was magical and knew God personally. I always felt safe & secure when she was around. When the summer came to an end and it was time to go to school, I could no longer travel with her, I was left with my grandfather and my uncles who were all in and out working. I was able to cook my own food, wash my clothes, iron them and get up on time for school every day.

  I was independent for a seven-year-old and I'd always been that way. Before my grandmother headed out to the airport, she told me to make sure I look after my mom and the kids. She told me to take them some soup and make sure they ate… and I did just that.

  One of my favorite shows was on television so I was glued to the tv and doing my homework at the same time when there was a knock at the door, it was the male cousin who lived down the street with my brother and sister. He asked was my uncle home and, in a rush, to get back to my show I answered "No, he's not here right now, but I'll tell him you stopped by." I kept looking back at the television so he asked what was I watching and could he step in to watch it with me until my uncle got back. He has come in before to watch wrestling with my uncle all the time and run errands for my grandmother so it wasn't unusual for him to be there, I said "sure okay but I have to get ready for bed soon, I have school in the morning." He sat in the rocking chair in front of the television and I sat on the sofa. About thirty minutes later, I'd finished my homework and the show was about to go off and he said "come sit over here" he was in a rocking chair so I looked up with a confused look on my face and asked "where?" He placed his hand on his lap and said "right here I ain't gonna bite you girl." I said I don't want to. He kept saying "just come sit on my lap it's okay you can see the tv better over here." I got up and I had never been more terrified, I barely sat on his knee and he grabbed me by the waist and slid me all the way in the middle of his lap. Tears began to come down my face as I knew it wasn't right and I felt so uncomfortable. I tried to get up and he applied pleasure and pulled me backward then forward then backward and then he opened his legs and I felt something between his legs as he kept pulling me on him. I asked him to please stop as I cried and he said "look at the television." I remember praying one of my uncles walked in the door or my grandmother called but no one called or came. All of a sudden, he wrapped his arms around me tightly and started rubbing on me like I was a grown woman as he made sounds. Shortly after, he removed his arms from around me and I jumped up and went to the front door. I said "I have to get ready for bed" he said "okay that was a good show tell your uncle I came by but remember our little secret if you tell anyone they will be mad at you and you don't want them mad at you, do you? So, I won't tell anyone if you don't." I shut the door and ran into the bathroom and got down on the floor and began praying as I was crying and trembling. I cried out for my mother, I cried out for my grandmother, but no one could hear my cries. I knew if I told my Dad he would kill him and I couldn't let my Dad go to jail, he and my grandmother were all that I had. I remember falling asleep in the tub trying to scrub the scent off me as this monster breathed all down my neck. I felt filthy and alone and I wanted to die in that moment as I felt it was the start of something far worse that even I couldn't control.

  Once a person touches you in an inappropriate manner and especially as a child, you are confused and afraid wondering "Should I say something?", "Will they believe me?", "Will I get in trouble?" All those things ran through my head and I didn't tell anyone what happened. I shut down and stayed to myself and I certainly didn't EVER want go back down the street or see that monster again.

    The following year or so we had a block party. My mom, grandmother and everyone was there. My grandfather was the block captain and always made sure we had a great time. I'd actually seen the cousin in passing and he spoke as if nothing had ever happened. He had started coming to watch wrestling with my uncle again and even went walking with my grandmother sometimes. He never tried anything like that again. I thought maybe he will never do it again and I even started blaming myself, suggesting that maybe it was something I said that made him do it. I knew it happened; I knew it was wrong, but I just wanted to forget all about it.

    My mom had been gone again for several days and I missed her so much. I knew that no matter what my mom did, she loved me although she didn't tell me, I always felt her love. My grandmother had even gone out to look for her in the middle of the night, but there was no sign of her. One afternoon, my uncle came in just as I finished my homework and said he just saw my mom down the street. My eyes lit up like a

Christmas tree and I wanted to see her so badly just to make sure she was okay. I really didn't think of anything else in that moment and headed down the street. I knocked on the door and the cousin answered the door and said "your mother downstairs and your brother and sister are asleep, come on in and I'll get her." I walked behind him and called out "mama it's me," but she didn't answer. He turned around and said "oh yeah that's right they just left" referring to my mother and my brother and sister's dad. My heart dropped and as I turned to go back to the front door, he grabbed my hand and placed it on his private area. I begged, "please no, don't do this again" he started to speak in third person "oh she don't want to play our game she want to tell and hurt her family" I said "no I don't want to hurt my family I just wanna go please." He said okay I'll walk you back home can you grab my jacket off my bed?" We were standing in the hallway where the basement was as well as the door to his room. My mom, brothers and sisters stayed in the basement and the cousin and grandmother rooms were upstairs. "Go on, grab my jacket." I could see it on the bed, but I really didn't want to grab it. I walked in and there were all kinds of books with naked people on them and an unforgettable scent of filth. "Never mind I'll grab it he said" and he came in and closed the door. It's like I was screaming internally, but nothing would come out. He started to speak in third person again and he said "let me lay her down, so she can relax" and he pushed me back on the bed. "Let me take her pants off. I'm not going to hurt her; I just want to see something." I began to cry and my chest felt like it was going to explode. I was usually the outspoken child as everyone knew, but at this moment I couldn't speak, I literally froze in fear. He was about six foot something and probably weighed a little over three hundred pounds. As I trembled, he grabbed my hand and made me touch his private area with tears flowing down my face, I begged him to stop and just let me go home. I promised not to tell or to never come back. I grabbed my clothes so tight to try to prevent him from attempting to undress me that my nails nearly cut into my skin due to my grip. Here I am a fifty-pound helpless little girl wrestling and fighting with this grown demon of a person for my innocence. He took my pants as well as my underwear off and he began touching me and looking back towards the door I guess to make sure no one was coming.

  He put his filthy mouth on my private area and he started to moan and groan, I threw up a billion times in my mouth and this sicko said "she taste good let me see something else" and I literally threw up everywhere and it startled him but he stood up still trying to undo his pants. He had one of the older doors with a key in it that you lock from the inside, I zoomed in on it and I decided even if he killed me, I was going to fight my way out. I jumped to my feet and fell as my pants and underwear were wrapped around my ankles. I got to the door and quickly turned the key and ran straight to the front door never looking back.

    I went running down the street barely breathing; and my legs and body were still in shock so much so that my body went completely numb and I collapsed by the time I made it to our front door. My uncles were not home so no one saw me. I ran to the bathroom and I probably stayed in the tub for five or six hours scrubbing my body until my light skin was completely red. I didn't come out until my uncle knocked on the door once he made it home and all I could say is "I'll be out in a second." I was scared out of my mind, I felt dirty and worthless and so embarrassed. I didn't want my uncles to see me like that. As I looked at the bruises on my body from the struggle and as my body ached, I wept so hard. I could still smell his filthy scent on me, but I made the decision to stay quiet until my grandmother came back or I saw my mom. I didn't care what happened this time, there was no question I was definitely telling my mom and my grandmother.

My Dad was supposed to pick me up the very next day, I planned to tell him as well. I ended up seeing my mom first and I was talking so fast and panicking as I told her that he touched me on two different occasions. I didn't even get a chance to go into details before she cut me off. She didn't say that she didn't believe me, but she certainly didn't say she did either. She went on to say "just stay away from him", and that she and the kids wouldn't have a place to stay if it all came out the wrong way. I thought "the wrong way" --this grown man hurt a child and he could hurt another child, my brother or sister even. I mentioned it to my grandmother as well when she got home. I remember her saying she would talk to him and make sure he stays away from me and that my dad would kill the cousin if I told him, so don't create confusion. My mother did confront him, but he denied it and said I must have been confused or something. I could tell his grandmother and mother knew that I'd accused him because they turned very mean and cold towards me and would no longer speak when I walked pass their house on the way home from school. His mother yelled out once to me when I was walking to my friend's house "you're a lying a$$ little girl and you should be ashamed of yourself." She would always roll her eyes at me and was just flat out mean and nasty towards me as if I had harmed her son instead of him hurting me.

The grandmother said I could never come there again which was fine by me. My brother and sister could come right down the street and I prayed I never had to lay eyes on that monster ever again. I couldn't believe my own mother would question me on something so serious. I knew my Dad wouldn't question me at all, but I never told him, fearing that if I called and told him, he would kill the cousin for sure and I didn't want my Dad to spend the rest of his life in prison. I had three sisters and a little brother at the time on my Dad's side and one of their mothers' was also on drugs. My Dad primarily took care of them, so I didn't want to put them in jeopardy of being without my Dad.

My mother gave birth again to another baby boy. Now she had three small children inside the home and all I could think of is that all three of them were at risk as the cousin was still living there with her, their dad and the grandmother. Sadly, although I expressed what took place it either wasn't taken seriously, or I simply wasn't believed.

Sexual abuse in childhood can definitely cause long-term psychological and social issues and that can surely carry over into adulthood and affect your married life and parenthood. Some immediate psychological consequences of child sexual abuse include shock, fear, anxiety, nervousness, guilt, symptoms of post-traumatic stress disorder, denial, confusion, withdrawal, isolation, grief, the list goes on. This is something that can leave you completely broken beyond repair. So many of us have experienced pain on an unexplainable level but we must find a way to begin to heal ourselves, if not we will find ourselves taking that hurt into our relationships, marriages, parenthood etc.

I went on to middle school, but my nights were long because every time I closed my eyes I either saw him or I could still smell his scent on me. I could've just curled up and died. I never slept with the lights completely off as I was afraid of the dark and nightmares were kind of like regular dreams for me. I would still climb in the bed with my grandmother and grandfather in order to fall asleep at night until my grandmother started giving me a scripture to read:

"The LORD is my light and my salvation; whom shall I fear? The LORD is the strength of my life; of whom shall I be afraid? Psalms 27:1 KJV

I recited this every night before I went to bed. It was as if it gave me a sense of peace in the midst of a terrible storm, I seemed to not be able to make it out of mentally. Although I felt lost, worthless and alone on the inside I never wanted anyone to know and for me it was better to not talk about it and just keep praying for a better tomorrow.

I didn't tell my friends what happened or my closest aunts and uncles, I spoke to no one else about it. Over time I carried a lot of hurt from the fact that my mother didn't do more to make sure I was protected as well as my siblings. I was angry because in my eyes she chose a man and drugs over her children. Not to mention I was never taken to the doctor to get checked out just to make sure I was okay. I was left to find a way to deal with it on my own as a child. It was never fully addressed as it should have been, and this monster was left on the loose to hurt another child.

My mother returned from another one of her three or four-day vacations and she stopped by our house before heading home, I hugged her and we talked briefly. She would always be so out of it when she returned and my grandmother always had food cooked and the blessed oil out and ready to pray for her. She said she was tired and going home to take a shower. When she got home and went downstairs, she walked right into the cousin in the physical act with my six-year-old brother! My mom immediately attacked him with a skillet and tried to beat him to death. I guess the angels of reality, strength and common sense came over her that night because she tried to kill her boyfriend with the same skillet once he came home. The police were called immediately, and the evidence was clear. This time he was charged with statutory sodomy and ended up ONLY getting sentenced to seven years in prison. I felt as though he needed the death penalty. I could still hear the sirens from the ambulance in my sleep for weeks and even months.

I was relieved that he was locked up, but I felt like I let my brother down and possibly my other two siblings if this monster had in fact ever laid a hand on them. It ate me alive that my little brother had to endure such pain. I dismissed the fact that I was a child myself around eight or nine years old when it happened to me the second time. I even said something to this sick individual's mother after it happened to me and she screamed at me, a child at the time. I later found out that she knew I was not his first victim and she didn't get her son help at all. Maybe if she had done so my brother could've been spared from the nightmare, he had to live through at the exact age I was when it happened to me the first time… seven-years-old.

My brother never really talked about it and all of my siblings grew older never knowing that I too was molested by their cousin. Although I was still a child and not the parent, I felt like I still failed my brother. I felt like I failed at protecting him, I cringed at the thought of what that sick monster did to him. I cried until my eyes hurt some nights. I felt as though this just couldn't be life. I wanted to take his pain away, I wished it were just me and never him who had to experience that disgusting nightmare. As I reflect, I realize that this dark time could have literally stopped me from living, it could have made me hate myself and give up on everything. After all, I'd had inner struggles for a very long time. No one believed ME when I said I was molested; it was ignored so no one cared right? This is what was on my mind when I laid down at night to go to sleep. I contemplated just leaving and never looking back; it crossed my mind many times and just made sense to me at the time. For a moment, even taking my life did as well, since at this point the only one truly looking out for me--was myself. But I wasn't going to take the coward's way out. I told myself if no one else cares, I know without a shadow of a doubt that God cares and he will never leave my side.

Yes, it was rough and some days it was hard to even pray and trust God. I questioned why I was handpicked to endure so much pain at such a young age. I was taking all that baggage to school with me every day and keeping it bottled up inside. Besides my great Uncle, who did a lot for me and took me wherever my Dad asked him to, I was also close with one of my other Uncle's on my Dad's side. He was my Dad's younger brother, very handsome and always well dressed like my Dad. He and his wife would pick me up from my grandmother's house, take me shopping, out to eat, and just spend time with me as often as they could. I never once shared what happened and what I was dealing with when they weren't around. I just threw myself into every activity and school event even more. While fighting tears daily, yet I was still giving it my all. I made straight A's, never missed a day of school, never complained, just kept going. So much had occurred in my personal life and all around me, so school became one of my main escapes. The more I started thinking about how my friends lost their mother due to a drug addiction, I began to have nightmares and visions of my own mother overdosing. I was fearful that my grandmother would one day get a call that my mom was dead. After the occurrence with my brother, I was hoping that would motivate my mom to clean herself up and get her life back on track. My brothers and sister never had the chance to see how beautiful and full of life our mom was before the drugs. I didn't sleep many nights as when I closed my eyes, I could literally see my mom in a casket. It was scary and so hard for me because I witnessed my grandmother saving my mom from being beaten and killed by one particular dope man, risking her own life and emptying her bank account. My mom survived being thrown from cars, getting severely sick as a result of the drugs and so much more yet she couldn't shake her addiction. I often thought about who would take care of my brothers and sister. Although I wasn't yet old enough to take care of them, I was determined to not let these challenges break either of us. My plan was to remove my brothers and sister from that house as soon as I was able to.

My Dad consistently picking me up on the weekends and he made certain that all of his kids had everything we wanted or needed. My Dad was the ultimate provider and my friends often called me lucky to have a Dad in my life, and one that pretty much gave me my hearts desires. Unfortunately, when "that" happened to my little brother I didn't feel lucky. I asked God why couldn't my brothers and sister have a Dad like mine, I wanted them to feel that same love and know that someone cares for them and that they were protected. Everything my Dad gave me I shared with them, but I couldn't fill the shoes of my mom and their father.

When a child is showered with gifts yet lacking love & support from a parent it can make or break that child. Sure, I enjoyed the shopping sprees my dad provided, the trips to big amusement parks and the "just because" gifts. But I must admit, as a young girl heading into high school soon, I was in desperate need of my mother's love and constant support and so were my siblings.

Be strong and of a good courage, fear not, nor be afraid of them: for the LORD thy God, he [it is] that doth go with thee; he will not fail thee, nor forsake thee.
Deuteronomy 31:6 KJV

Chapter 3
Pushing Pass the Past

Acknowledging yet overcoming the pain from your past.
Not allowing "what was" to define you.
One of our greatest accomplishments is being able to face our past with no regrets, turning our tears of pain into tears of joy, recognizing the true winner within.

It's not easy to push pass the past. You must have something that drives you, keeps you pushing and hoping for a better tomorrow even if it's just the thought of knowing it will get greater later. You must have a WHY. In my case, at that time my drive was my siblings. My younger brother started to get into trouble since there really was little to no supervision for them. Our neighborhood was declining, crime was at an all-time high and witnessing a drive by shooting up close or a drug transaction was still the norm. I wanted better for my siblings and I knew I had to tuck away all my emotions to make it out of the "hood" so the three of them could see more than yellow tape around a dead body.

Some days when I opened my eyes I remember looking up, thanking God that I was still alive although something inside of me felt dead already. Have you ever felt like screaming but nothing would come out?... like running away and never looking back ...just wanting to desperately find yourself but you feel too lost to find your way? That's how I felt EVERYDAY but I never wanted anything to be all about me, my hurt or my struggles. I just wanted to save everyone else from being on the receiving end of the type of pain that I had experienced, that leaves you broken and empty. I wanted to live and not cry myself to sleep at night. I had to figure out how to do that; how to save myself. I asked my grandmother and my dad if I could move in with my aunt and uncle after my first year of sixth grade. They lived in a better neighborhood with better schools, so I thought getting away for a while would help me mentally and maybe offer better opportunities academically. It was bittersweet, because my brothers and sister still lived with my mom and their dad up the street from my grandmother. A huge part of me did not want to leave them, but it was necessary in order for me to attempt to heal myself from the constant reminder of having a mother--yet not really having one and feeling like filth every time I had to, continuously, lay eyes on that monster, after he hurt me. With all that going on inside of me and keeping it to myself, I developed stomach conditions and started to have migraines a lot. My Dad and grandmother took me to the doctor several times, they ran several tests on my stomach because I was always sick and could only eat and drink certain things. However, the doctors never found anything. I read a lot back then and most of my symptoms lead me to believe that I was basically severely depressed. Again, I kept it all to myself and I was just eager for a new start at a new school. My friends went on to a different middle school as well and I truly missed them, especially my best friend but we always kept in touch.

    The move with my aunt and uncle turned out to be a great decision. My aunt was gorgeous and very classy. You could certainly tell she and my mom were sisters. She was married with one son when I moved in and her husband had been around since I was two years old, so he was as close to me as my other uncles were, actually a little closer. Since moving in with my aunt, my middle school years were definitely much better than before the move. I was able to focus more on my love for writing. Of course, I was involved in every activity the school had to offer. I had even earned a spot to go on a scholar trip to Boston that my dad paid for. Flying to Boston would be my first time ever on a plane and traveling without family, but I looked forward to the experience of something good for a change. The move with my aunt and uncle was like a breath of fresh air. I made many new friends but I grew really close to one in particular, she and I walked home from school together every day. The crossing guard grew fond of us and would greet us every morning with "there go my guhs" not girls. He reminded me of my grandfather a lot and we felt safe walking knowing that he could see us coming and going. As I said, things were going well and I was just happy that I actually was able to get rest at night for a change, no sounds of gunshots, no nightmares and my stomach pains began to ease up a little as well. I felt like God was hearing and answering my prayers.

    I still visited my grandmother's house on the weekends and my dad's on alternate weekends. I was able to spend time with all my siblings on both my mom and dad's side and I loved them all the same. I never believed in the "half-sister or half-brother" thing, we were all blood and we all resembled; some more than others. We grew up loving and supporting each other and my dad often stressed the importance of us being united and staying close no matter what. My dad was the coolest, best dressed man I knew, and he always smelled good. He wore the best cologne and loved the finer things in life. This is probably why I loved to dress up, wore suits and loved Elizabeth Taylor perfume at the age of seven. My dad never remarried once he and my mom separated, so for years he took care of four girls and one boy by himself without missing a beat. My aunt, my dad's sister came over and helped out. She combed our hair, cooked and cleaned the house. However, my dad was something like a renowned chef in his own right and he could cook anything from my favorite meatloaf to seafood pasta with every ingredient from scratch. His presence was constant in my life, as well as all my siblings. He provided all that we needed and more, involved himself in all of my school affairs, and set the bar pretty high for me. Honestly, at times I wasn't sure if I would ever live up to all of his expectations. It was not that I was incapable, but because I still carried so much on the inside and had some battles to face of my own. God knows I wanted to talk to my dad about it all as I knew I could, but I couldn't bear the thought of letting him down in any way. I pushed pass my own insecurities and gained strength from his motivation, his guidance and his everlasting support in everything that I did. I woke up one day and wanted to model and do beauty pageants so he had my uncle drive me to three different states to compete, do photo shoots and train if necessary. I was never met with "Mika you can't do this...you can't do that" it was always "Okay babe your daddy's working but I'll make sure you get there and have everything you need". I was indeed a daddy's girl and I hung on to his every intelligent word for as long as I can remember. He told me that you have to work hard for what you want, never give up on your dreams and as long as you can acknowledge what your goals are in life you will achieve them. My Dad owned and operated an ice cream/ convenience store as well as a soul food restaurant. When I was about thirteen, I worked at my dad's ice cream & convenience store on the weekends. I did a little bit of everything ranging from keeping the books, stocking shelves and assisting my oldest sister as a cashier. When my dad first decided to open the store, he said he wanted it to be the community's store and not just sell snacks & ice cream. He wanted it to have immediate necessities that one may need but maybe couldn't afford sometimes. The importance of giving and spreading love to others was something he lived by. He pretty much adopted the neighborhood kids and was a huge provider to all of his brother's and sister's children. He always treated them as his own. Many of our cousins stayed the whole summer with us and a few even lived with us. My dad took on more of a father's role instead of an uncle's role to several of my male cousins. This was his charismatic, selfless character, always putting the needs of others before his own and never looking for anything in return. He didn't always get the acknowledgement he deserved in my opinion, but he was never looking for kudos from people. He once told me "As long as God is pleased with you, you're good babe." His faith in God wasn't expected by some because of his outer appearance. He wore super nice clothes, jewelry and had a few gold teeth, but once he spoke you knew you weren't dealing with an ordinary guy. Also, his car never moved without his bible on the dashboard. I always asked a million questions and he would answer every one, but only after laughing so hard at some of the things I would have the nerve to ask him. He just had a way of making everyone feel special. He showered so many with love, gifts and his knowledge of the world. I witnessed grown men get excited just to be in his presence, truly a legend in my eyes and many others. My dark days were overcome by all the time I spent with my dad; he shared a lot about his past with me. He talked about every job he ever worked and what it took to get where he was. He told me how determined he was to never allow his past to define him, but instead he was focused on making his future and that of his children better. I never saw a man who loved his children so much and did everything within his power to keep a smile on their faces. It was his drive and encouragement that helped dry my tears from things he didn't even realize I was hurting from; it was my dad who told me I will be one of the best attorney's and or leaders the world has ever seen one day. I received hope and the push I needed just knowing that he had such amazing confidence in the woman I would one day become.

It's a blessing to have someone be the light that you need in your darkest hour. God will preserve you even as a child. Some of us have been hurt far worse than others but there is a purpose behind all of the pain. When you are on the receiving end of the neglect, hurt, and abandonment it's hard to see the light and walk in positivity. Throwing in the towel seems so much easier yet something within you will not allow you to bend or give up. When a person strips you of your identity and takes your innocence away leaving a piece of their filth on you that's hard to scrub away it can rob you of your will to live, your joy, your peace and even your ability to identify what happiness looks like anymore. It can make you look in the mirror and hate the reflection you see. It makes you feel as though you are living with those broken pieces and the thought of being unsure if you can ever put them back together again can break you. Well… breaking is NOT an option, but gaining your inner strength back and being determined to live and free yourself of ALL the pain and disappointment IS an option.

I can do all things through Christ which strengtheneth me.
Philippians 4:13 KJV

Chapter 4:
Overcoming

Recognizing your challenges, looking at what tore you down and finding the strength to build yourself up again. You are an Overcomer.

As long as we continue to live our lives there will be a storm to weather. It's not about how strong the winds are or how much damage was caused, it's about the fact that you are still standing, and that you've survived. God can never get the glory if we don't have a story. Overcoming is a huge accomplishment and you must survive your test in order to give your testimony. My grandmother would say "you have to go through the wilderness to get to the promised land baby" and this stands to be the truth. With tears on my face and anger in my heart from life's experiences at such a young age, I was still determined not to fail. My dad's love, my grandmother's support, along with their prayers and mine were my strength to prevail. I will never say that it's easy to keep pushing your way when enduring a storm but giving up gives the enemy and those who brought pain into your life power over you. Our past shapes our future, but it's important not to allow our past to define us and understand that we have to break the chains once and for all and demand peace and greatness over our lives no matter how ugly it once was. Sometimes it takes reflecting on our past to soothe the pain and brokenness in the present.

Every day I woke up ready to beat the "odds" and reverse the so called "statistics." I continued to work hard and go to school every day, still determined to strive for the very best. I was very active in school. I was class president, president of the student council, an honorary member of the national vocational honor society, you name it I was a part of it.

When I moved in with my aunt and uncle, I started to spend a lot of time with one of my closest cousins who shared my love for school and lived near my aunt's house. Although we were cousins, we really were best friends and we dressed as twin cheerleaders every single year for Halloween. (You would've thought that was the only costume that the store sold). She played basketball and was much more athletic than I. Alternatively, I loved to write and was much more outspoken than she was. We stayed up talking and laughing all night when we would sleep over at each other's house, but not once did I burden her with what I'd been through when I lived with my grandmother. Upon completion of my three years of middle school, I started high school at the same school my cousin attended. She was one year older, so I was a freshman and she was a sophomore. Half way into the semester a representative from a technical school came to visit our high school. They offered a two-year financial services/accounting program that I decided to enroll in at the beginning of my sophomore year. It was the perfect opportunity for me as I'd kept my father's books in order at his store for quite some time and I grew to have real passion for finance & accounting. This was a no brainer although I still had the dream of becoming a defense attorney one day. The school provided transportation, but the only downfall was I had to move back with my grandmother full time to be near the bus route. I wasn't thrilled about moving back and I knew I would miss my cousin, the normalcy I had finally adapted to and I would also miss all the talks my aunt and I had. My aunt was my idol and the time I spent with her and my uncle was a lifesaver. I was so grateful to them for inviting me into their home and caring for me like their own daughter. Their oldest son and I were more like brother and sister than cousins, they all just made me feel welcome and loved and I will forever love them for that.

I moved back with grandmother later that summer and I was ecstatic about starting school in the fall. Sleeping in my old bed at my grandmother's house stirred up a few memories, but I tried not to leave time or space for thoughts of the not so happy times from my past to resurface. I mainly stayed focused on my future and how this new school and program can help me to achieve some of my goals. I greatly missed the new friends I'd made, but I was also happy to be reunited and close to my best friends. Most of my friends had boyfriends. I just told myself I didn't have time for boys. Besides, I knew my dad would never go for that although my oldest sister was dating at a much younger age than I was. I wasn't looking to "date" anyone and I mostly stayed in my own little bubble except on the weekends. I spent time with my friends and I went to church with grandmother consistently. However, like most young girls who after watching Cinderella and the Little Mermaid, I started to dream of having a prince charming and falling "in love" one day. I actually kind of fell in love accidently with one of my childhood friends' cousin. I say accidentally because although I'd known him just as long as I knew her, I never looked at him as anything more than her cousin. He moved out of town with his father to Detroit a couple of years prior to me moving back to my grandmother's but would come home to visit during holidays and the summer. Whenever he came in town we would all hang out at their grandmother's house, go to the mall or the movies, just teenage summer fun. He became my very first boyfriend. The first two years of our relationship was long distance and although I'd known him since elementary school, I was still extremely shy around him. It took me a while to accept gifts from him, eat in front of him and I surely wasn't ready to kiss him yet. I knew most of my friends were already sexually active, but I wasn't quite ready for that and wasn't sure when I would be considering the trauma from my past. I never shared any of the details regarding the dark times in my life with him at that time, but he respected my decision and waited until I was ready. He graduated high school and received a baseball scholarship to college but ultimately ended up moving back to St. Louis while I was finishing my last couple of years of high school. At this time, I was still living with my grandmother and he was living with his mom just a few blocks over. We went from having a long distant relationship, to seeing each other every day. I couldn't believe I had fallen for him to be honest as he was my complete opposite. However, he was very sweet and always trying to find ways to make me smile. My grandmother wasn't too fond of him at first because she heard that he was a gambler and led a fast life but once she met him for herself, she saw something different in him and gave her stamp of approval. He was a jack of all trades, he could fix anything, was a wiz in math, and his drawings would leave you to believe he had an art degree. He started accompanying me at all family functions on holidays and as time went on my aunts, uncles and other family members viewed him as family and they really liked him. Everyone got along very well with him, everyone except my dad. I actually waited a while before I even mentioned him to my dad because I knew he would disapprove and think that having a boyfriend would interfere with my studies as well as my future. Just as I predicted, he wasn't happy at all and he actually was a little more upset to learn the news than I'd expected. He didn't ask many questions about who he was, his family, where he's from, what did he do etc. He said he knew all that he needed to know and that he wasn't the right one for me. He said it in such a tone as if that were the end of it and he'd better never hear of this guy's name again. Of course, it hurt me badly because this was now my boyfriend, but at the same time this was my dad. I always valued his every word, but I did not think it was fair that my older sister had already dated several guys and he would not give just this one a chance for me. I'd never disrespected my dad or went against his word so when he demanded I stop seeing him I said okay I hear you and I understand dad, but I never actually stopped seeing him. I went home and told my grandmother what my dad said and I cried my eyes out. I even said something to my mother when I saw her and asked if she could talk to him for me. Their relationship was still a bit estranged although they were still legally married yet separated for many years now. My grandmother told him that she had her reservations at first but he turned out to be an okay guy and he seemed to really care for me as I did him. I tried all that I could; but he was not having it, so I pretty much hid my relationship from my dad and regretfully went against his word. I figured he just needed time to get to know him and then he would see he was a great guy with a bright future ahead of him.

  Meanwhile, I was finishing my senior year and preparing for graduation. I found it to be unbelievable that this was my last year before I started college and I was actually going to be the first female in my immediate family to graduate from high school. Lord knows I worked hard and dedicated all of my time and energy into school, and I just felt like it was finally all paying off. The light of positivity was starting to show up in my life and I was learning to throw away the fake smile and truly wear a smile on my face and heart that was real. The first semester of my senior year came to an end and everyone was preparing to leave for Christmas break. My senior advisor informed me that final grades were in and I actually had enough credits and the option to graduate early. She went on to tell me that my G.P.A. was a 4.0 and I was currently number one in my graduating class, which made me valedictorian. She also shared that my classmate who was also in the same financial services program that I was in, ranked number two and was the salutatorian. However, she made it clear that if I graduate early, I would basically forfeit valedictorian to the salutatorian. My advisor said although I had no other classes to complete, I could work in the office and it would satisfy enrollment to still hold my place as valedictorian. All my friends were planning to get new jobs, go on trips or just relax and hang out at the mall until graduation. Honestly, I could've used a break and Lord knows I loved to shop and spend time with my friends but I thought to myself after all it took for me to get there, all the blood, sweat and tears, there was absolutely no way I was just giving my accomplishments away, just to be able to able to leave school early to "chill" until graduation.

  I didn't even speak to my dad or grandmother about it, I knew what choice I was making the moment I walked out of my advisors' office. I returned in January after the holiday break and worked as an office aide during school hours. I discovered that it wasn't bad at all and

I was able to work closely with my principal and assistant principal on numerous projects. That summer, a week before my graduation my mom randomly came to me and said she wanted to get help and get in a drug rehab program. I was surprised to say the least, but ecstatic of course. I hugged her and reassured her that I would be there with her every step of the way. Things were truly beginning to look up and I couldn't wait to walk that stage in a week. I was so excited! All the graduation festivities were set! Just a few days before graduation we received a call that a terrible tragedy took place and my boyfriend's brother was murdered back in Detroit. It's crazy because his brother had recently visited, so we had just seen and hung out with him. He and my boyfriend were only a year apart in age. Learning of his brother's murder tore him and his family to pieces as expected. He had lost his uncle a short time before and that took a toll as well, but this was his brother and they were extremely close. It was his brother who first told me that my boyfriend liked me and jokingly told me "you better give him a chance". We all had been around each other since grade school so he was definitely family to me. My heart ached terribly for his loss. I did not have the right words to say, so I just prayed and told him it will get better and we will get through it together. He had to leave town for the initial funeral arrangements where he, his dad and brother all lived before he moved back after he graduated. A second service would take place the following week once they all returned, but it broke my heart that I wouldn't be able to be by his side out of town as my graduation was just a couple of days away.

My mom relapsed for the millionth time and was nowhere to be found on my graduation day and truthfully, I expected it. Nonetheless, I graduated as North Tech's Valedictorian class of 2001. As I gave my speech and looked out into the audience at my family's faces there were all kinds of emotion falling over me. It was hard not seeing my mom's face, the fact that my boyfriend wasn't able to be there, I wasn't able to be there for him during this trying time of losing his brother and just standing there reflecting on all the hurt I'd overcome. There was also a feeling in the pit of my stomach that made me want to scream "Thank You Jesus I Made It" after all that was thrown my way I did it! When I looked into the crowd and saw my dad take off his Cartier glasses and wipe tears from his eyes smiling from ear to ear, it made my heart happy like never before and in that moment, I was ready for the world and looking forward to my future.

"Let not your hearts be troubled: ye believe in God, believe also in me. In my Father's house are many mansions: if it were not so, I would have told you. I go to prepare a place for you. And if I go and prepare a place for you, I will come again, and receive you unto myself; that where I am, there ye may be also.
John 14:1-3 KJV

Chapter 5
Daddy Knows Best

Someone else's expectations of our lives may not look identical to the picture we've painted for ourselves, yet we will find that sometimes their frame may fit better than the one we've chosen.

  I enrolled in Harris Stowe State University immediately following graduation and I figured I'd start my law journey, so I majored in Criminal Justice with an emphasis in Psychology. My first year was beyond successful, I made the dean's list maintaining my 4.0 GPA and my dad was so proud of me. He told me he'd already put the money aside to send me to Law school after I graduate. I received tons of scholarships which covered 80% of my tuition but my dad paid for everything else including my books, supplies, clothes and accessories. He was just that kind of dad. My school was about ten minutes away from my dad's store, so I still worked there after school or just stopped by to tell him all about my classes and my day in general. Nothing gave me more joy than knowing I was making him proud; I was so afraid of letting him down as he was always my #1 cheerleader.

On the other hand, my boyfriend and I continued to date and my dad was aware of it now, he truly knew all along although he still didn't like him, mainly because he said he knew he was a "wanna be playa and he don't deserve my daughter." He didn't like him or the thought of "Mika" dating. It didn't matter that I was now eighteen or that I always stayed on the positive route despite my environment or the actions of others around me, my dad just had a view for my life that he was sticking to and that view did not involve a boyfriend.

My boyfriend was aware of how my dad felt and during the rare moments when they would be in each other's presence he would try all he could to show my dad he wasn't who "the streets said he was." My dad knew of one individual very well who my boyfriend viewed as an uncle and hung around quite often. The fact that they were connected was enough for my dad to be certain he would never be what his daughter needed.

It was a struggle for me because I loved my dad with everything in me. I just wanted him to see that we can't judge others based on what we've heard, we must go by what we see in that individual. I knew that nothing I said or did changed his feelings, he just reluctantly let it be.

We were young but we talked about our future a lot and how adamant we were about getting our families out of the hood and one day living in our dream home. I stayed focused on school while trying to decide which law school to attend. He was musically talented and a great writer. He decided to pursue a rap career in hopes of the opportunity to write for others. I personally thought he would re-enroll in college and pursue engineering or even become an electrician as he had the skill set for both.

The things we had in common most was that we were both cut from a different cloth than those around us and we shared the love of helping others. I always felt as though whatever we did we would be great at it because we had the each other's support. At this point we had been together for five years, were inseparable, and still stayed on the phone until the sun came up like when we were younger. We started talking a lot about getting our own place together. However, I knew that the next time I left, I wanted to make sure I could take my younger sister went with me. Although, I wished I could take all three of them.

My younger brother was in and out of trouble at the time which ultimately landed him in the juvenile detention system. He was labeled the "rough" one of us four. I could see right pass all that toughness on the outside right to the sweet and charismatic little boy on the inside. My other brother who was the twin to my sister on the other hand was still in school and he was literally known as the neighborhood young handyman. He could fix everything from bikes to TV's, you name it and he would fix it. He was so intelligent and handsome. Although he and my sister were twins, I always said he was like a male version of me. My younger brother and sister who barely got along when they were younger, were more alike than they'd ever like to admit.

My plan was to move them all away to experience a better environment with positive opportunities and that included my mom too however, she wasn't ready to leave and declined my offer. She agreed that my sister should go with me since she was the only other girl. We actually had a written agreement through the court that awarded me legal guardianship of my sister. I was nineteen by then, working two jobs, in my second year of college and I told my boyfriend once we moved into our new place my sister was coming along with us. Later that summer, I ended my apartment search and found the perfect two-bedroom townhome for us. I was so excited, yet it was bittersweet that I would have to leave my grandmother. She and I were like two peas in a pod and she was truly my rock. Even with my dad still not fully on board with my relationship with my boyfriend she was always supportive and speaking up on our behalf, trying to convince my dad to take the time to get to know him for himself. Although my mom and dad were now finally legally divorced my dad still called my grandmother "mama" and she remained one of his closest confidants over the years.

It did bother me deeply that I couldn't just go to my dad and talk about my plans for the future like one day wanting to get married and have children once I graduated and started my career. The fact that I was getting ready to move into my first apartment, I knew he would be head over hills happy for me yet not happy about who I would be sharing all these things with. I knew how proud he'd always been of me, this was the first and only thing he wasn't proud of and God knows it broke my heart but at the same time I felt like I needed to follow my heart. I was in love and my boyfriend was the only guy I'd ever been with. I never even dated anyone else before him. As time went on, my Dad tolerated him and would hold short conversations when he picked me up from working at the store. Nonetheless, it was still something about him that wasn't pleasing enough for Dad to sign off on him completely; and for to me bring up the possibility of marriage was surely out of the question. I figured I'd give it time and get ready for the move into my very own first apartment. I looked forward to a new beginning and the smile it would put on my sister's face and heart.

I still couldn't believe that I managed to graduate high school, complete my first year of college, and move my sister and I into a nice and peaceful two-bedroom townhome. I was so grateful to God for keeping me in the midst of every storm. All I knew is that everything prior was to prepare me give my siblings a better life and meet every goal I had set for myself. My immediate family was super supportive. My aunts and uncles helped out a great deal as well. My dad and my uncle were responsible for me having my own car since I was sixteen. My dad bought my first one and my uncle bought my second one. Eventually, my dad gave me a nice truck that he had gotten customized just for me once I started college, so I had more than enough room to pick my brothers up on the weekends. I spent time with all of my siblings, like I said before, I wasn't raised calling my siblings on my dad's side "half brothers or sisters" we were all blood and even my brother and sisters on my mom side felt the same. I had a total of seven siblings, four sisters and three brothers. Although I was the second oldest of all my dad's kids, my older sister treated me like the big sister. This was fine by me as I was used to taking on the motherly role, not to mention all of my grandmother's friends called me an old soul.

Life was good at this point, my relationship was getting stronger, my sister was adjusting to her new school and doing very well. My grandmother finally decided she was ready to leave behind what she and my grandfather started over thirty years prior. The neighborhood was getting worse, so she was also ready for change. She actually found a cute two-bedroom condo within walking distance from where I'd moved, so it was perfect and that made my heart smile as I needed her close to me. My mom and other family members still lived in our old neighborhood and my sister went to stay with my mom some weekends to spend time with her, her dad and our brothers.

One weekend I dropped my sister off and I told her I'd pick her up on Sunday as I normally did. My boyfriend and I spent the weekend shopping and enjoying our time alone. He always went out of his way to show his love for me. Jewelry was his favorite gift of choice. I remember when we were younger, he bought me just because gifts and offered me money all the time; but I wouldn't accept it. My aunt said I was crazy for not taking it, but I was extremely independent and always worked for everything I wanted. Plus, my dad still spoiled me even as a young adult. I appreciated all the gifts he gave me, but didn't want to feel as if our relationship was built on material things. I wanted to know that the love was real. He actually gave me a promise ring when I was seventeen and we talked about marriage nearly every day from that day on.

    We were so sure that we were each other's forever and to us we were the perfect match. We'd dealt with not only my dad having reservations about our relationship but some of his family members weren't truly fond of me either in the beginning. However, his dad and I were extremely close and he was always genuine and kept it real with me. After all, I had known him since I was a little girl and he called me "daughter in law" from day one--not once did he ever call me by my first name. He still lived out of town but would come visit from time to time and he often stayed with us when he did.

    I decided to get my sister a new bedroom set and surprise her when I picked her up from my mom's the next day. I knew this would make her really happy as this would be the very first time she had a bed of own. I called and told my mom about the bed earlier that day and let know her what time I'd be there the next day. Later that night my mom called and told me that my sister was rushed to the hospital and according to the paramedics she'd had a seizure. My heart was racing as we rushed to the hospital. I had no knowledge of my sister ever having a seizure before and was beyond frantic. I started to pray as tears fell down my face. It was difficult for me to keep calm and I began to regret letting her go to my mom's in the first place.

  Once we arrived, I spoke to the doctors and found out that as a result of a fall she'd suffered a year or so prior while sitting on the back of a parked car, the head injury from that incident was likely to have caused the epilepsy. Once she was stable, we all went in to be by her side. I told her how sorry I was that I wasn't there to comfort her and that I'll never leave her side again. She was twelve and I'm sure this was scary for her as it completely freaked me out. The doctors said she would be okay, but I had to meet with the specialist in the morning to know exactly how to deal with it in the event she has a seizure at home. It was kind of a surreal experience. I couldn't hear the doctors anymore; my head was spinning and I was overwhelmed and needed some air. I went out to the car and my boyfriend came behind me consoling me, telling me everything was going to be okay. Before we arrived he told me that he had something to tell me but once I received the call I totally forgot about it, so as he's holding my hand and we were sitting in the car I asked him what he wanted to talk to me about earlier? He said never mind it can wait, but I insisted that he tell me right then especially if it was good news, Lord knows I needed it.

He was still hesitant, so I turned to him and said "seriously what is it"? My heart nor my mind was prepared for what he was about to say to me. With tears in his eyes he told me how much he loved me and how he has never loved anyone else as much as he loved me and I'm perfect in every way, but he made a terrible mistake. I remember swallowing really hard and turning my head away from him, my heart felt like it was going to explode. Here I am sitting in the hospital parking worried about my little sister and you tell me how much you love me and so on so forth, yet you made a terrible mistake? Then he said it… "I got someone pregnant."

Do you remember your favorite boxing match that you either saw in person or on television and the champ served his component with a "one hitta quitta" and knocked him out? Yeah, in that moment with all kinds of emotion running through my body, I felt like I'd been in a boxing ring for all 12 rounds and took a mighty blow that resulted in the knockout of all time. You couldn't have paid me to believe he was getting ready to tell me such a thing after all we'd been through; not to mention I had just gotten the most frightening news ever, we're at the emergency room and my twelve-year-old sister could have died. There were so many emotions and thoughts running through my head, but I couldn't utter a word. I pulled myself together and went back upstairs to be by my sister's side and played everything off in front of my family not mentioning a thing. I didn't say anything else to him while we were there. I focused on my little sister.

On the way home I asked him how he could do this to me, how he could look me in my eyes and lie to me constantly with the fake I love you's and I can't wait to marry you etc., knowing the ultimate sacrifice I made going against my dad's wishes to still be with him. I told him I stood by your side through everything, putting our love first. He interrupted me and said "Mika you know I meant it when I said I love you and I still want to marry you baby it was a mistake, please know I never meant to hurt you." I told him I was done and didn't want to hear it. I spent some days away at my aunt & uncles house to clear my mind and my best friend came over to be with me as well. I just remember crying and thinking how could I have been so stupid, how could I have believed in such a liar. It was a very difficult time to say the least, but I had to find a way to live with the choice he made and decide what I was going to do. I thought about all the opportunities I had to go away to college with full ride scholarships, just how different my life would've been had I listened to my dad.

  I still wasn't talking to him too much and if I did, I kept the conversation short. One day he went and bought a ring, got down on one knee and proposed. He went on and on about how this female being pregnant wouldn't change anything with us and how he told her he was in a relationship and even paid her to get an abortion, but she wouldn't get one. He was trying everything he could think of to win my love and trust back. Meanwhile, some of his family members were planning a baby shower in he and the mother's honor, despite he and I supposedly still being in a relationship. No one knew of my choice to take a break from the relationship, but those closest to me. Those days had to be some of the roughest days for me and I can only blame myself "for we are warned before destruction" and my dad certainly warned me, but I didn't listen.

  Around the time that the baby was due, I couldn't reach him at all, and I called around looking for him. I remember his family being so cold to me over the phone almost like an "ah ha" that's what you get. I know some were happy this was taking place in hopes that we would break up once and for all. I was in a state of shock and disbelief. We had furnished our home, decorated together and made so many plans. I couldn't grasp what was happening and I couldn't believe my life had taken such a turn.

After searching for him most of the day, I was driving in the rain and now it was dark. I began to think of what my dad would say and how he would react. I thought about the true feelings of others as it related to our relationship. My mind was just all over the place as I was driving, crying and filled with so much anger. Suddenly, I heard a horn blowing loudly in front of me and when I looked up cars were coming towards me. I had somehow veered over onto the wrong side of the road. I snapped out of it, pulled over and began to pray asking God for strength and guidance as I was clearly losing it and allowing the actions, dishonesty and cruelty of others to get the best of me. I could have been in a tragic car accident and died that night and I know that God sent an angel from heaven to be by my side and shield me, I couldn't stop shaking and Thanking God and I never told a soul about that incident.

The next morning, he came home and told me the baby was born and although he had prior reservations, he now knew the baby was his but he still wanted nothing but for me to be his wife. We talked, cried and talked some more and in my mind, this was the first and only boyfriend I'd ever had. We had been together at that point for six years and we were living together with joint bank accounts. No, there's no justification for disloyalty and it's never okay for someone who claims to love you to hurt you so deeply; but when you're young and think you're in love you follow what you believe to be signs from your heart and you find yourself forgiving them. The pain and embarrassment never goes away and you find yourself settling on hope and promises. He begged and pleaded for forgiveness. I know that didn't mean I had to forgive him, but despite his mistakes I was still deeply in love with him; so I accepted the ring and we started planning a wedding.

But they that wait upon the Lord shall renew their strength; they shall mount up with wings as eagles; they shall run, and not be weary; and they shall walk, and not faint.
Isaiah 40:31 KJV

Chapter 6
Holy NOTrimony

The importance of waiting on God & being ready for marriage.
Were they your soul mate or was it your soul you allowed them to take?

Sometimes we think we have it all figured out, we begin to plan our lives according to OUR wants, not realizing that God will allow us to get in our OWN way when we don't allow him the right-away over our lives. This is just to teach us to never interrupt his plan for our lives and proceed without his approval again. It's SO important to allow him to truly order your steps, wait on him and stop trying to force something that was never meant to be.

Every girl has dreamed of marrying their prince charming. We've pictured ourselves all dressed up in a beautiful flowing wedding gown, looking our very best and surrounded by our family and friends. We picture ourselves celebrating a beautiful union with the one we love, the one we've decided to spend the rest of our lives with. We look forward to all the happiness in the world seeing only what we want to see and blocking out everything else.

We can have all the signs in the world that suggests we should not to be with a person, and yet we will paint a picture of our own. We do this knowing its faker than a $3 bill, but still we create a fantasy hoping it all pans out. In the words of Maya Angelou:
"When someone shows you who they are, believe them the first time."

We often make the mistake of wanting to see or find the good in people so badly that we accept the worst from them.

There were certainly signs when I began to plan my wedding, but I pretty much ignored them all, mostly gut feelings and just knowing he wasn't ready even though he insisted that he was.

The day before I decided to tell my Dad about my wedding plans, I found out I was pregnant with our oldest son. I prayed for Jesus to be a fence, and for mother Mary and the disciples to come down and help me deliver this news. Lord, I had knots in my stomach, I'm talking knees shaking and everything. It was not out of the ordinary for me to pull up to my Dad's store and he and I sit out in the car and talk for hours, so I called and told him that I was pulling up in five minutes. I got in the car with him and he asked how school was going and had I decided between the two choices we'd talked about for law school once I graduated from undergrad next year. We continued small talk and I turned towards the window and proceeded to tell him about the pregnancy and the wedding. I was sure to mention that I'd already spoken to my advisors and wouldn't miss a beat at school. I would actually get done earlier than expected, have the baby then start law school the following fall semester. I was talking so fast, barely breathing, I could tell he was upset but he didn't yell at all (which he never did) but I started crying telling him I was sorry and please don't be disappointed in me. I still couldn't turn to look at him. This was my number one guy and although I was excited about getting married and becoming a new mother, I felt like I let him down. He said "Mika, babe you're smart, nothing about you is ordinary and I knew that when you were born, your Daddy knows your worth and I want you to marry someone who knows it as well". He congratulated me on the pregnancy, but it was clear he still wasn't feeling the whole wedding idea. He proceeded to tell me that my oldest sister told him about my soon to be husband having a baby with someone else. Yeah, you could've just bought me for a penny, talk about feeling like "boo boo the fool." That was certainly a reminder to me that my Dad was right about it all. But there I was, determined to see the good in my man no matter the signs that were slapping me upside my head. I told my Dad no matter how it looked today, I WILL still make him proud.

    We had a huge engagement party and all of our family attended. I was sporting my three-month baby bump and we danced and had great laughs all night long. My Dad began to come around little by little but certainly still had his reservations. Nonetheless, we planned a destination wedding in Jamaica, but it ended up feeling as though we were eloping when it ended up only being the two of us in attendance. My God Mother accompanied me to the bridal shop to pick out a dress and all she said was "Be sure this is what you want lil girl." She was very outgoing and fun to be around with a sense of humor like no other. I had my dress, he had his tux, we had our rings, so we paid for our trip to Jamaica and were ready to become husband and wife.

    I was taking five classes at school trying to finish my Bachelor's degree, coming home taking care of my sister and keeping things together as I prepared to give birth to my son. I started noticing little things that suggested my fiancé at the time, was still cheating. Someone would play on my phone day and night and say things like "It's gonna break your little heart once you find out" then they will hang up. He started staying out later and later, sometimes until the next day and when I questioned him, we would argue and he would say "They just want your spot, everyone knows who has my heart and they're just jealous." He wasn't a drug dealer, but he gambled whether it was on the boat or at the local pool hall. I had stayed out late plenty of nights with him so he told me "Baby you know what I do, I'm not out here with any females, I'm trying to take care of us, you gotta trust me baby." I naively believed his every word. He dropped me off at church on New Year's Eve, normally we would've attended together but I didn't exchange words. He told me he had to meet up with someone who owed him money and that he would pick me up later. When church was over, I called him but I didn't get an answer. My grandmother and I ended up leaving church together and she dropped me off at home. I called him a few times once I got settled, still no answer. He called back eventually and said he'll be home soon, but he was very short with me. My gut told me that he was with a female and I had a hunch who it was.

  I fell asleep a little after 2 am, and there was still no sign of my soon to be husband. My phone rang a little after 4 am and when I said hello, his cousin was on the other end of the phone screaming to the top of her lungs. When I was able to make sense of what she was saying, I learned that the father of my unborn child was shot multiple times including once in his head and was on his way to the hospital in the ambulance. Hearing he was shot in his head hit me like a ton of bricks and it felt like my heart stopped for a minute, I didn't know what to expect but I began praying immediately. I was seven months pregnant with my first son and the thought of losing his father was unbearable. I rushed to be by his side, of course. My best friend was there with me and two of our other childhood friends as well.

After being in a coma for nineteen days, God saved his life and restored him completely. The doctors witnessed a true miracle as he was shot at close range in his head, stomach and leg. This caused him to go through several intense surgeries, had pins inserted in his leg and was limited to a liquid diet for quite some time. I didn't care what took place with us prior to this incident, he was still my soon to be husband and the father of my unborn son. After being at the hospital sitting and thinking for days, then weeks, I started to put the pieces of the puzzle together. It turned out my intuition was right the night he was shot. I learned the identity of the woman he was allegedly with at the time he was shot, and it turned out that it was her boyfriend who nearly killed him. His first couple of days in the hospital, this particular woman showed up with his cousin who called and gave me the news the night he was shot. I actually saw a picture of him kissing her while looking through his phone for a picture of his insurance card. It all started to make sense. He woke up after two weeks of being in a coma and immediately began to apologize, telling me how much he loved me and that he would never throw away what we've built for seven years for anyone. He said that no other woman was as worthy as I was. He also told me that he had a talk with God and that as soon as he heals, we will get married, raise our son and put all of this behind us. I didn't leave until he was discharged which was exactly 26 days later, one day before my birthday.

    I slept on hospital chairs for 26 days—pregnant. I met with the entire team of doctors every morning and watched closely so that I would know how to care for him once we were home. He came home on an IV and I had to change every dressing for all his wounds, give him blood thinner shots, his medicine through the IV, you name it--I did it and nursing was never an occupation I desired to have. Don't get me wrong, I think the men and women who choose that field are truly disciples of God, but I never thought I had the stomach for it until someone I loved dearly needed me to play that role. I eventually had to drop my classes and push them back to the following semester. It was one of the hardest decisions I've ever made, but I knew I would be right back at it a couple months later and walking the stage with my degree the following year. During his road to recovery my life long prayers were answered, my mom was delivered from her drug addiction and she and my two brothers moved in with us temporarily. She began helping me a great deal. This meant the absolute world to me and I was so grateful to God for turning her life around and even more excited for my brothers and sister. A couple months later I had my son and my husband to be was healing up quite nicely. He went from using a wheelchair, to walking with crutches, **physical** therapy and eventually walking by himself with a slight limp. At the end of that year right before Christmas, we flew to Jamaica and got married.

When I got married at the age of twenty-one, truthfully speaking I wasn't fully healed at all from the hurt I endured during my childhood or my broken relationship with my mom. I was grateful for her efforts to stay clean and being willing to rebuild our relationship. I prayed before we exchanged vows that God blessed our union and that anything that had taken place in our past remains there and that he leads and guides us to building a strong foundation for our family. I never said "Lord your will be done" I never asked "Lord is this the husband that YOU have for me" nonetheless, we exchanged ``I do's" and I was now a mom and a wife.

My mom ended up getting married later down the line and my brothers and sister moved in with her and her husband, he was truly a nice guy and treated us all as if we were his own. The oldest of my two younger brothers, could still fix anything he put his hands on and his smile and goofiness made you love him.

My younger brother was a bit rebellious growing up, but he was still my baby. To this very day, I still call him "newborn". He was the youngest, but he wanted to protect us all. My sister was pretty chill, I always told her I thought she would be a great nurse because of her charismatic side. She was also very attentive and she had my mom's smile. I was so excited that they finally had a chance to have a real family with no drama and my mom was present all the time. Her husband worked hard and was a great provider. Life was finally good for them--therefore I was good.

My son was growing so fast and I LOVED being a mother. The one thing I noticed during my marriage is that somehow, I had silently accepted the fact that I might get hurt because I was used to a couple forms of hurt already.

My husband and I had known each other for most of our lives prior to getting married, but he didn't become aware of the abuse from my childhood until later on in our relationship. I never experienced physical abuse in my marriage, but I did begin to experience a form of mental abuse. During the time that someone started playing on my phone, someone was also apparently stalking me; driving around our neighborhood and I had no idea. One of my classmates was a police officer in the area we lived in and he stopped this same woman due to someone calling about a suspicious car in the neighborhood. She told him that my husband was supposed to be with her, and not me. She said that he promised he would leave me, but he's taking too long and she can't live without him. This sounded like a fatal attraction movie from Lifetime. I think I was in a state of shock and denial when he called and told me to please be careful because the woman seemed very unstable. This woman was originally introduced to me as a "cousin," then I find out she was the cousin's friend, and eventually turned out to be the girl whose boyfriend shot and left my husband for dead on New Year's Day. Well apparently, he never stopped dealing with her and they were in a relationship according to what she told the police officer. One time, she had the audacity to knock on my door, my mom answered thinking she was a Jehovah

Witness and my husband ended up making her leave before I even realized what was going on. She also made sure that I knew that his mother and sister were well aware of their relations for years and that she had a great relationship with them. Did I mention the fact that this same woman attended our engagement party? Yeah, I should've been in my orange jumpsuit BUT GOD. I went to bed with devastation and woke up to humiliation for fourteen of the nineteen years total that we were together. I gave birth to my second son right in the midst of all this turmoil. There were certainly more women and several cases of infidelity throughout the marriage. Some would be so comfortable that they would call me after he'd spent a day or two with them and tell me "He loves you and the kids so I don't know why I deal with him." They would tell me if it was his mom, sister or cousin that brought him to their house, what he wore or whatever. At least two of the women had his name tattooed on them and one of them actually thought I was a mistress and the good ole stalker was the wife. Honey, this was a real live Jerry Springer show. I'll never forget when I was eight months pregnant with my second son, I climbed on top of an air conditioning unit outside of my husband's friend's apartment (don't ask me why) and caught him and one of his side pieces in the act. Let's just say after running my pregnant butt around that complex, I couldn't get my hands on her but I tried to knock him into Jerusalem after he tried to make me think I was crazy and told me I didn't see what I thought I saw. He was with the one that I called "the email girl" because I don't know if it was her conscious or what, but she would email me every time she cheated with him. She confessed that she was the one I saw through the window during my spider girl act on top of the air conditioning unit and even told me that she ran and hid at the top of the steps that's why I couldn't find her. He still denied it. My marriage was a full -blown circus.

    I was married, yet I felt alone for the majority of the marriage. The infidelities did not move me as much as the lack of general support through some of the most traumatic stages of my life. He and I were friends first, or so I thought. I never expected to be hurt by the person I exchanged vows with and had known for years.

Love is patient, love is kind. It does not envy, it does not boast; it is not proud. It does not dishonor others, it is not self-seeking, it is not easily angered, it keeps no record of wrongs. Love does not delight in evil but rejoices with the truth. It always protects, always trusts, always hopes, always perseveres.
1 Corinthians 13:4-7 NIV

Chapter 7
Tragedy & Trials

Sometimes the bad things that happen in our lives put us directly on the path to the best things to ever happen to us…

It seemed trials was more my middle name than Andrea. I decided to focus on finishing my degree and making more money so I could do something special for my brothers and sister. My younger brother ended up in the juvenile system and that knocked the wind out of me. I was trying so hard to save them from the system in every way. He was so tough on the outside, but I know he suffered a lot of hurt on the inside and all I wanted to do was save him from himself so he wouldn't self-destruct.

I started a very successful mortgage business with a friend and built a brand-new house a couple years later. My twin brother & sister were entering their senior year of high school the following year. I was so excited to tell them about the house and invite them to move in with me. Although things were going good with my mom, I wanted to help them both get ready for college. We were set to close on our new home on Dec 22, 2006. I planned to surprise everyone around Thanksgiving with the news of closing.

On Sept 4, 2006 around 7:35 pm I received a call that my brother had been shot and I needed to get there quickly because it wasn't looking too good. I arrived on the scene with my family and we were told my brother was pronounced dead on the scene. At that very moment I could literally feel my heart shatter into a million pieces, and I couldn't breathe or halfway speak. I could hear my mom screaming to the top of her lungs, my grandfather weeping and praying, my Gany trying to keep things under control and calm everyone down, but we were standing on the street where we all grew up; looking at my brother's lifeless body lay on the ground and there was nothing any of us could do to bring him back.

I felt helpless all over again and I glanced up the street at the house my brother & I were both abused in and I began to tell him how sorry I was for not saving him and not doing more to protect him. I told him how much I loved him and that I was not at all ready to let him go. We still had colleges to visit to decide where he was going and to pick out his décor for his new room at the new house, I didn't even get the chance to tell him the surprise. I was crushed. My little brother couldn't respond to me, I couldn't see that smile that lit up the room anymore. A week later I had to plan his funeral, dress him and have his homegoing then figure out how to live without him. He was only Seventeen years old with a bright future ahead of him, yet his life was tragically cut short. At that point I didn't even want to finish building the house, it felt like it was pointless.

    Meanwhile I tried to turn to my husband. I was even willing to still fight for our marriage. I was hurting and just couldn't endure anymore pain, I needed him. When so many preys on your downfall and against your marriage/relationship it can create a hurdle that's sometimes too hard to get over. The infidelities continued with the old fling and a couple of new ones and we began to grow further and further apart.

    On June 30, 2008 I received a call that turned my world as I knew it upside down. I was told that my Dad was followed home from his place of business, robbed and shot. I remember so vividly dropping to my knees and asking God was this some kind of never-ending nightmare?! Did I do something wrong? Why is all this pain coming back to back? My Dad, my number one supporter, my EVERYTHING. He could not leave me, there's no way--he's like my oxygen. Who would harm a man that helped EVERYONE?! He took care of his family, the community, strangers and probably his enemies. I just couldn't believe this; I just knew whoever called me had it all wrong.

During the entire drive to my Dad's house, I just kept saying I CANNOT LOSE MY DADDY! I just knew I couldn't lose him; I wouldn't survive that as I was still grieving for my brother. I attended church regularly with my grandmother and I'd been praying all my life. My Dad never drove his car without his Bible on the dashboard, so prayer was real to us and I surely had Faith, but I was terrified of the thought of losing my dad. I was screaming on the inside and pleading with God. My sister and I arrived at my Dad's house and my soul left my body when the officer stated that we couldn't go in the house because my Dad was gone. Gone??! I asked the officer, "You mean he's gone to the hospital?" He said "No, I'm sorry, he didn't make it." I had no feeling in my body, no words that I could speak; I wanted to die at that very moment. I wanted my Daddy, and like my brother he was taken from us so tragically. This was not right! I was angry! I wanted answers. Our youngest brother was just a toddler and would have normally been with my Dad. I was consumed with the thought of him growing up without the opportunity to witness how GREAT of a man my father was and how much he loved his children and took care of us all. He never said no to anything I ever asked for, he treated all of us as if we were royalty and we were because we were his and he was certainly a King.

    Suicidal thoughts were present daily, my heart was so broken and I was so lost without my Dad. I no longer had that support that I received from him; I didn't trust anyone as I trusted him. Everyone had hurt me in some kind of way but he never hurt me; he would always tell me "Mika babe you can run the world, you deserve the best, you're too smart to settle for anything." I now understood why he was never a fan of my husband because he knew he would hurt me. When he heard things about him cheating on me and having a baby with another woman, I could see the pain in his eyes because he knew my husband's actions had hurt me. He never disrespected him; he just knew that his daughter deserved better. It made me sick to my stomach that I couldn't tell him I was sorry for not listening when he tried to warn me before I got married. I just couldn't believe that he was gone.

    After my Dad's death, I was so numb I didn't care if my husband stayed gone three days or three weeks. I didn't care about what was going on around me. I was so broken and confused that I couldn't see straight. My cousin whom I call "my favorite," left her home and came over to spend days with the kids. Sometimes she stayed for a week at a time. I wasn't mentally present at all. God sent her to be my side and save me from having a mental psychotic breakdown. I love her so much for that. I had two sons at that time, and they saw their mother struggle through some mighty dark days. My health started to go downhill, my partner and I had to close the mortgage company and my dream home went into foreclosure. I ended up filing for divorce in 2009 but didn't go through with it especially after my husband and I lost one of our close childhood friends to gun violence less than a year after my Dad passed. He was like a brother to us both. My husband took it very hard and I comforted him for months as this loss awakened the pain we both suffered at the loss of both of our brothers'. As I look back, I was always the one providing all of the comforting through every situation. It seemed no one was ever there to comfort me or dry my tears. So I just held onto the words my grandmother always told me…" You're not responsible for how others treat you but you are responsible for how you treat them."

  I gave birth to a healthy, beautiful baby girl in May of 2012, so I tried to give the marriage another shot. Our marriage had simply run its course a long time ago; but have you ever kept trying to breathe life into a dead situation? Yeah, that's exactly what it was. I filed for divorce again in July of 2014 and it was finalized in Sept of 2014. All within the year 2014, I lost my job, my grandfather, two uncles, went through divorce and had to move in with my grandmother for a couple of months until I found a place. The kids and I went from living in an almost 4,000 sq. ft. home to a 950 sq. ft. apartment, but the peace I finally had was priceless.

Although I finally freed myself from the marriage, there always seemed to be another trial waiting around the corner. I ended up going through a total of four emergency surgeries including kidney surgery and two surgeries to remove masses that were suspected to be cancerous. Imagine a doctor calling to inform you that the MRI suggests the mass on your shoulder was indeed cancer while your three children are in their room asleep. I didn't pick up the phone to call anyone. The only thing I did was fall to my knees and cry out to God for hours and speak life and healing over my body. That day I said I'm done with all the stress; I won't take anything else for granted. I will operate in Faith and not allow anything or anyone to knock me down so low that I forget just who God made to be. Yes, I felt like I'd been through hell and back and that's pretty much the truth but considering all that I had been through, every diagnosis, every pill bottle for depression, anxiety and every sleepless night for four years, God kept me in the midst of it all. The pain I endured showed me how strong I really was. My marriage ended but I didn't resent my Ex-husband. I told myself you can either come out BITTER or BETTER and I chose better. We are friends to this day. I had to make sure there was no bad blood between us because I needed to be free from my past so I could welcome my future. In order to do so I had to forgive him and learn to forgive myself as well. I had to learn to trust my process and truly allow God to order my steps.

Consider it pure joy, my brothers and sisters, whenever you face trials of many kinds, because you know that the testing of your faith produces perseverance. Let perseverance finish its work so that you may be mature and complete, not lacking anything.
James 1:2-4 NIV

Chapter 8
A Look in the Mirror

*Taking a look at self.
Forgiving yourself and those who hurt you ... pressing forward.*

In the midst of your personal storm when it seems like everywhere you turn there is turmoil, the very ones you expected to "love" and protect you specializes in hurting you. Many that you called your "friend" turned out to be your foe. Before you can catch your breath, tragedy rips your soul from your very body, and every time you take one step forward it's like you fall five steps back. No matter how many tears you've cried and how many people have single handedly tried to destroy you, you cannot give up! I know throwing in the towel seems easier, discouragement has set in and you may even want revenge on those who harmed you, maybe you want to give up on life but it is at that moment when God will step in and rescue you from the fire. He will restore your strength and literally make your enemy your footstool. He will Bless you in the presence of the very people who preyed on your downfall using every brick that was thrown at you to build you back up. Though you walked through the fire, he did not allow you to get burned.

Time was up, I had waddled in depression long enough. I was over all the prescriptions, constant anxiety attacks, migraines, not being able to eat and walking around like a zombie. I would perk myself up just before my kids came home from school so I could make dinner and help them with homework. That had become my daily routine. I started thinking differently after giving birth to my daughter and still trying to make my marriage work. I asked myself, "Is this the example I want to be to her?" "Do I want her to think it's okay for someone to mistreat her and not value her as the woman she will one day become?" I wanted my daughter to know that she should be treated like nothing less than a Queen. It was her and God who gave me that final push I needed to file for divorce and actually go through with it. My children were worth more to me than anything.

It took me a very long time to let go of my past. I spent 19 years in a relationship that was built on lies and deceit. I honestly didn't want to feel like a failure by walking away and I felt as though I had already let my Dad down by staying in the relationship so I might as well try to force it to work. The problem is…. you can't force or fix a thing that is already broken beyond repair. I know that now. I learned that you can do everything right….cooking, cleaning, taking care of the kids, being a REAL mother, run his bath water, iron his clothes and you can swing from the ceiling fan and bring every fantasy to life in the bedroom….if a man wants to cheat they STILL will. My lesson learned is that a man will only do what we as women allow. A man will change for a woman he genuinely loves, and he will not hurt you. I have no regrets because my personal storms made me the warrior that I am today. God was my anchor and he pulled me through even when I wanted to drown. I took a look in the mirror and I told myself, you deserve better. Admittedly, there was a point I didn't like the reflection I saw because I was broken; but in my brokenness I found my healing. My three children were and still remain my WHY. They saw me at some of my weakest moments. It was time they saw me in some of my strongest. Losing my Brother, Dad, Uncle and my Granddad left me numb. Though I was reminded of the strength they all instilled in me, I felt like a piece of me died when they left. My Dad, as intelligent as he was, would call me before he made investments or any business decision because he had so much faith in me on every level. He trusted me. It was time I had faith in myself.

God has a way of sending you a light during your darkest hour, and he did that for me. Ladies what I will tell you is, when a real man shows up to love you, LET HIM.

Whoever caused you any pain, as hard as it is you must forgive them for the sake of your own peace & happiness. It doesn't mean you've excused what they've done but you have transferred that power back to you. Remember your peace is PRICELESS. Grudges and Resentment can block your blessings. No one played the song "Resentment" and "Bust your windows out your car" more than I did. I was ready to go tear the club up out of anger and humiliation when I was going through my marital storms. After a while I said to myself, I will feel a whole lot better if I let God fight these battles for me because trust and believe everyone who has a hand in putting a tear on your face or an ache in your heart has to come face to face with karma and meet their maker. Let go and Let God.

You must divorce your past in order to marry your future. It's a fact that you can mess your entire life up loving the wrong person. We must learn to wait on God to send us who he made to love us the way we deserve to be loved. We must learn that every test and every trial is necessary. You have to tell yourself that I am no longer holding on to toxic relationships, friendships or family members. Once someone costs you your peace--you know you have invested way too much! Say to yourself, I no longer have space for anything that's not beneficial to where God is taking me. Take it from me, I once was blind but now I can see that I survived what should've killed me. I was Sabotaged but I was set FREE! We are in control of that reflection we see in the mirror. We can soak in our sorrows or turn our sorrows into success. My grandmother used to say "You're too Blessed to be Stressed and Too Anointed to be Disappointed." The days of giving someone power over you and allowing them to control your happiness is over. Oftentimes we give others the key to our happiness not realizing that we've been robbed. Well, it's take back season! Take back EVERYTHING the devil thought he stole from you. It's time to put YOU first and not be afraid to love on yourself because you are Worthy.

I praise you because I am fearfully and wonderfully made; your works are wonderful, I know that full well.
Psalms 139:14 NIV

Chapter 9
The New YOU: Push, Pull & Strive

Let Go & Let God.
Let go of your past & Get Excited about your future.

Hurt people, hurt people. Especially when they haven't dealt with the traumas in their own lives. Stop blaming yourself for someone else's wrong doing and making excuses for why they hurt you. Ask God to remove anything and everyone who doesn't mean you well according to HIS journey for you. God has a plan for your life, it doesn't matter who hurt you, or broke you down, what matters is who or what made you smile again.

It wasn't easy for me to pick up the pieces and put my life back together, but I started with putting me first. I'd always put others before me, but not this time. My first order of business was to finish my degree. I didn't care how many years had passed, I had to do it for me. I not only finished my Bachelor's degree, but even after being discriminated against at a reputable university, I pushed right past that and earned my double Master's degree two years later. My mind, body and spirit went through so much trauma, but I was determined to still make my Dad proud and push for my dreams because I was tired of losing. I also learned what true love looks and feels like. I will never make the same mistakes again. I know my worth. I only want who and what God wants for me. I Found My Happy and I intend to keep it.

Now that you've taken back everything the devil "thought" he stole from you Push to the limit and go after your dreams.

Set your plan into action and never look back. You are in control. Allow Happiness to walk into your life & stay there. Exhale, you made it out of the storm, and you can now embrace the NEW YOU.

Live Your Life Because IT IS GOLDEN, Let Nothing or No one Ever Steal your Joy Again. Find your Peace, Find your Happy and KEEP it.

Trust in the Lord, and do good; dwell in the land and enjoy safe pasture. Take delight in the Lord, and he will give you the desires of your heart.
Psalm 37:3-4

My Mom & Dad before I was born in 1981

My Mom & I

My Gany & Grandfather who raised me

My Gany

My Dad & I at my 8th Grade Graduation

My Aunt & I

My Mom

My Dad & I at my High-school Graduation

My Children & I

In Remembrance of ...

My Father Lemuel "Pookie" Houston Jr.
My Grandfather Andrew Johnson Sr.
My Grandmother Creola Houston.
My brothers, Corey Patrick Sr. and Cleophus "Buddy" Robinson Jr.
My uncle Clinton "J.R." Bohannon.
Charles "Lollie" Jones Sr., Randolph Ingram Sr. and one of my biggest supporters, Frank "Pops" Jackson II.

ACKNOWLEDGEMENTS

"For EVERY mountain, you brought me over, For EVERY trial, YOU saw me through, For EVERY blessing, Lord I THANK YOU!!! For THIS I give YOU praise!!!!" LORD I owe it ALL to you. When I was drowning, lost and confused it was YOU who pulled me through. Thank you for saving me time and time again showing me unspeakable Favor.

To my Gany Lula "Bell" Johnson, I know you're rolling your eyes; due to the fact that I'm telling the world your middle name. You can't stand for me to call you that, but I never told you why I've always loved your middle name; it's because in my countless darkest hours I was saved "by the bell" and that was YOU. Thank you for introducing me to my Lord and Savior Jesus Christ and teaching me not only how to pray, but how to get a prayer through. You are my best friend, my life line and I Thank you from the bottom of my heart for EVERYTHING.

To my Mom, thank you for showing me Strength & Determination. To my Godmother, Aunts, Uncles, My Siblings & My "Circle", I love you beyond words and your love & support has meant the world to me.

To my Mume, "They cannot count us amongst the broken" Lord knows you've been my rock and I love you for loving me.

To my children; PJ, Dame & Haleigh, my babies, you have seen me in some of my weakest moments and you've witnessed some of my toughest storms but always know that it was you who gave me the strength to stand strong and fight through it all. You all are so wise beyond your years, so incredibly talented and beautifully Blessed. I'm so grateful to God for allowing me to be your mother. Everything I do is for YOU. To my God children Mariah, Elijah & Nylah, I'm so honored to be your G-Ma; you have all been three incredible blessings to me. I want all six of you to Always Keep God first & know that you have the Victory over any situation that comes your way. You are Kings & Queens who will do GREAT things in this life. I Love You all.

To My Readers ...

Bear in mind the Hebrew scripture "Now faith is the substance of things hoped for, the evidence of things not seen. Hebrews 11:1 KJV Yes, it's sometimes easier said than done--but our faith is as important as the air we breathe. Sometimes God will shake your foundation, allowing you to be broken and stripped of everything just to show you and remind you of who you are and whose you are! You have a purpose;

God's had a plan for you since the day you were born and I don't care how much "they" continue to drag your name through the mud and deliberately sabotage you, know and understand that when the smoke clears you will be able to stand and say "I have fought the good fight, I have finished the race, I have kept the faith." 2 Timothy 4:7 NIV. You are getting ready to go from the Pitts to the Palace. Many of us are forced to live with daily reminders of who hurt or broke us down. However, the reality is what matters most now, is who or what has made us smile again. Ultimately, through all that pain & suffering… here we stand.

    If you've endured pain in the past or currently enduring any kind of pain, abuse, betrayal, tragedy, anxiety, grievance, depression, self-doubt, or any daily reminders, I want you to know that whatever hand you were dealt in this life wasn't meant to break you, it was meant to MAKE you! Trust me, as crazy as it sounds, everything you've been through was NECESSARY according to God's plan for your life. Please understand that I know just how hard life can be. It will knock you down, drag you through the mud and then throw you away. I stand with you claiming love, peace & victory over your life, for you ARE an overcomer and more than a conqueror. I am a living testimony and I can assure you that there is calm after the storm, a broken heart can be healed, and whatever the enemy brought up against you to destroy you and kill you WILL make you stronger. Life can be rough, and the people you thought loved you the most can be your greatest torturer. But even in your darkest hour, God WAS and IS still right by your side. Therefore, you have the victory and you've already won the battle. My journey wasn't easy, but I made it. Now it is time for you to Find & Keep Your Happy.

ABOUT THE AUTHOR

Tamika Andrea is a force to be reckoned with. Born and raised in St. Louis, MO she's a natural born leader who's always had a deep love for helping and uplifting others. The spiritual guidance and leadership that she gained from her grandmother has kept her grounded during some of the most trying seasons of her life. The Bachelor's and Master's degrees she's earned would be in vain if she couldn't master the art of forgiving those who hurt her, learn to walk in her true purpose and be exactly who God called her to be. Although she's endured many tests and trials, when she looks in the mirror, she now sees Strength, Perseverance, Courage, Determination, Power, Peace & Happiness.

Tamika is a mother of three beautiful Children and three amazing God children. She turned her Sorrow into Success; she took the bricks that were thrown at her to build something no one can ever tear down again. She forgave herself for not loving HERself first. She ran all the red lights until she finally found her Happy and now, she's ready for the best chapters of her life.

"Once you've determined your worth and know what you want in life, you don't settle for anything else." -Tamika Andrea

www.ingramcontent.com/pod-product-compliance
Lightning Source LLC
Chambersburg PA
CBHW042312150426
43200CB00001B/3